CW00545594

'I love this book! Beautifully ar
wasted word, it is full of hope
autism, for their resources ar
with people with autism, ther
why you should not own this b...
— *Guy Shennan, independent consultant in solution-focused*
practice and Chair of the British Association of Social Workers

'Belongs on the shelf of everyone who works with people with autism. It gives both practical and thought-provoking ideas for all practitioners, not just solution-focused ones. The authors are thorough, knowledgeable and accessible in their writing.'
— *Dr. Fredrike Bannink, clinical psychologist and*
author of 1001 Solution-Focused Questions

'I highly recommend this book. Its major contribution is its clear illustration of the strategies and application of an alternative treatment approach to people with autism; in contrast to the classical "problem-focused, symptom-based" model, the authors illustrate a solution-focused, strength-based paradigm.'
— *Dr. Ronald E. Warner, clinical psychologist and*
founding director of the Solution-Focused Brief Therapy
certificate program, University of Toronto

'Simply, clearly and concisely written, explaining much that is a mystery to non-autistic people. The authors show us how autistic people think, how to phrase our questions, how to use visual communication methods, and much, much more. Their passion for work with autistic people will inspire professionals to take a solution-focused approach in their work with autism.'
— *Judith Milner, co-author of multiple books on solution-focused*
practice including Creative Ideas for Solution-Focused Practice

'Well-presented and readable, with clear and practical examples. For me the highlight is the importance of its use of positive language, and the necessity of following your client's inner-directed needs.'
— *Ioannis Voskopoulos, psychologist, TNA Clinic*

AUTISM AND SOLUTION-FOCUSED PRACTICE

of related interest

A Self-Determined Future with Asperger Syndrome
Solution Focused Approaches
E. Veronica Bliss and Genevieve Edmonds
Foreword by Bill O'Connell
ISBN 978 1 84310 513 8
eISBN 978 1 84642 685 8

Using Solution Focused Practice with
Adults in Health and Social Care
Judith Milner and Steve Myers
ISBN 978 1 78592 067 7
eISBN 978 1 78450 325 3

Creative Ideas for Solution Focused Practice
Inspiring Guidance, Ideas and Activities
Judith Milner and Steve Myers
ISBN 978 1 78592 217 6
eISBN 978 1 78450 497 7

Helping Adults with Asperger's Syndrome Get & Stay Hired
Career Coaching Strategies for Professionals and
Parents of Adults on the Autism Spectrum
Barbara Bissonnette
ISBN 978 1 84905 754 7
eISBN 978 1 78450 052 8

AutiPower! Successful Living and Working
with an Autism Spectrum Disorder
Herman Jansen and Betty Rombout
ISBN 978 1 84905 437 9
eISBN 978 0 85700 869 5

Working with Adults with Asperger Syndrome
A Practical Toolkit
Carol Hagland and Zillah Webb
ISBN 978 1 84905 036 4
eISBN 978 0 85700 192 4

AUTISM AND SOLUTION-FOCUSED PRACTICE

ELS MATTELIN AND
HANNELORE VOLCKAERT

Edited by HANNAH COOK

Jessica Kingsley *Publishers*
London and Philadelphia

First published in Dutch as 'Oplossingsgericht aan de slag met mensen met autism a.n.d.e.r.s.' by Garant Publishers, Antwerp-Apeldoorn

Published in 2017
by Jessica Kingsley Publishers
73 Collier Street
London N1 9BE, UK
and
400 Market Street, Suite 400
Philadelphia, PA 19106, USA

www.jkp.com

Library of Congress Cataloging in Publication Data
Names: Mattelin, Els, author. | Volckaert, Hannelore, author.
Title: Autism and solution-focused practice / Els Mattelin and Hannelore
    Volckaert.
Other titles: Oplossingsgericht aan de slag met mensen met autism
    a.n.d.e.r.s. English
Description: London ; Philadelphia : Jessica Kingsley Publishers, 2017.
Identifiers: LCCN 2017000825| ISBN 9781785923289 (alk. paper) | ISBN
    9781784506445 (ebook)
Subjects: | MESH: Autistic Disorder--therapy | Autistic Disorder--psychology
    | Autistic Disorder--diagnosis
Classification: LCC RC553.A88 | NLM WS 350.8.P4 | DDC 616.85/882--dc23 LC
record available at https://lccn.loc.gov/2017000825

British Library Cataloguing in Publication Data
A CIP catalogue record for this book is available from the British Library

ISBN 978 1 78592 328 9
eISBN 978 1 78450 644 5

Printed and bound in Great Britain

CONTENTS

PREFACE

This book is based on our experience of working as professionals with people with autism. It is rooted in solution-focused thinking – the firm belief in the possibilities of every human being, which implies a respectful, emancipating and pragmatic approach of assistance and therapeutic work.

The solution-focused professional is a facilitator who focuses on the possibilities, talents and resources of people rather than on their problems. As a result, clients are able to experience a sense of ownership and responsibility and can begin to believe in their own abilities.

Els Mattelin has been working with children, teenagers and adults with autism for 14 years. Her experiences, way of thinking, approach to study and some wise lessons she has learned along the way are the foundations of this book. Hannelore Volckaert is a remedial pedagogue with a great deal of experience assisting adolescents and families.

Els and Hannelore discovered that they shared styles of working and a philosophical approach during their training as solution-focused therapists, and as a result they joined forces in vzw Dynamiek in Izegem, West-Flanders, Belgium. This organisation was started by Els after she had noticed there was a significant demand for specialised assistance for (young) adults with autism. Time has proved that indeed there is a big need for this sort of social and therapeutic work, and that the approach and know-how of Els' organisation is unique.

It is not an obvious decision to work with people with autism in a solution-focused way, as this approach implies that you set aside the problem and focus on what the client wants instead. This strong, pragmatic and future-oriented approach requires a lot of abilities that are not necessarily evident for people with autism. And yet we notice that this method is working and that people with autism find it incredibly valuable. Thus, it turns out to be an ideal method for supporting people with autism, provided one takes into account the particular characteristics of autism.

Over the years Els has developed and recorded some specific applications, the result of which you are now holding in your hands.

THE BASIC IDEA

A lot of people with autism tell us that professionals such as social workers or therapists treat them as persons who lack abilities and knowledge. Without asking, though frequently with the best of intentions, people take control out of their hands. This is often frustrating. The person concerned feels patronised and robbed of having a say about what happens to them. A solution-focused professional tries to avoid this at all times. We always look for what is already there, without judgement, but with a lot of wonder. And this can be a source of hope for people on the autism spectrum.

In this book we will not provide extensive information on how a solution-focused method works. Instead we refer you to the excellent literature that has already been published on the subject. However, to find this book useful, you do not need a thorough background in solution-focused theory. We provide abundant examples, so you'll notice quickly if this solution-focused method suits you. If we have made you curious, we have taken our first step.

Experience has taught us that solution-focused ways of working can be of help to people with autism who also have mental health issues. Thus we have included examples of autistic people with and without mental health issues.

In the DSM-5, new diagnostic criteria are given for ASD or 'autism spectrum disorder'. However, our starting point when working with people with autism differs from this. We understand autism as a way of thinking and experiencing reality that is very different from that of neurotypical people. That's why we use 'D.I.F.F.E.R.E.N.T.' as an acronym to structure our interventions.

The fact that DSM-5 refers to autism as a 'disorder' implies a prejudice and lifts people without autism to the level of 'normal'. If we approach people with autism from within this framework of standards, we are not helping them; we do things that are not effective; we impose solutions on them that do not apply; and we fail as therapists, social workers and professionals.

We believe that treating people with autism as fundamentally different people, without any judgement, is a principal requirement for being able to work with them in a correct, professional, respectful and effective way. That is why in this book we refer to 'people with autism' exclusively, and not to ASD or any other 'disorder'.

Els Mattelin and Hannelore Volckaert

PART I

THEORY

OUR UNDERSTANDING OF AUTISM

Based on our working experience with people with autism and a lot of research, we have developed a comprehensive framework for understanding autism and the differences between people with autism and people who are not autistic. As a result, we often hear our clients say that they 'finally feel understood and are able to be themselves' during our conversations.

We may want to take it for granted that clients feel understood within a therapeutic context, but for people with autism this is frequently not the case. Therapists, counsellors and other professions may reach out to them with the best of intentions, but they rely on a set of standards that do not fit for people with autism. In other words, because professionals depend on a (non-autistic) worldview and on (non-autistic) ideas about the needs of people, they often intervene in a way that is not adapted to the specific needs of people with autism. We have learned that this way of working is not effective. If you want to work successfully with people with autism, it is crucial to understand how these people live, think and respond to experience.

For example, we noticed that social workers, parents or partners of people with autism are often concerned that people with autism may be socially isolated because they appear to have so few friends. If, however, somebody with autism feels perfectly happy with just one close friend and a few contacts on social media, who are we to judge that this cannot be sufficient for a good and meaningful life?

Furthermore, studies indicate that people tend to find more and better help in therapy or assistance when they feel understood, and it goes without saying that this applies to people with autism as well.

This is why we find it necessary to share our understanding of autism, how we relate to our clients and their contexts to this particular framework, and how we work with them accordingly. We believe this is very important because our experience has revealed that autistic as well as non-autistic people find it difficult to comprehend what autism really means, what makes people with autism different and what this entails for their daily life and relations.

THE ESSENCE OF 'BEING DIFFERENT': THINKING IN DETAIL

The core manner in which people with autism differ from others is in how they think and perceive the world. Their way of taking in information, of using their senses as well as a specific way of processing these stimuli (by thinking), is different. People with autism see, hear, feel, smell, taste and use their senses in a manner that focuses a tremendous amount of detail, and their thinking is based on these details. The consequences of this should not be underestimated: imagine seeing your whole world in details, feeling and experiencing nothing but detailed information, and thinking accordingly!

In an attempt to explain to our clients with autism and the people close to them how this detailed thinking works, we like to use the schematic drawing in Figure 1.1. Although it simplifies reality, it can help to get the picture of what it is that makes people with autism different.

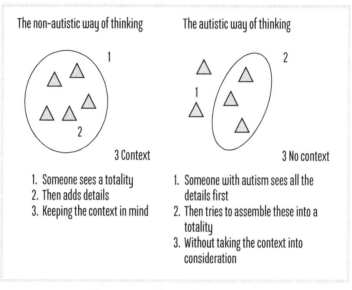

Figure *1.1   Non-autistic/Autistic*

Compared to those of us without autism, people with autism perceive things in a very fragmented way. They tend to focus mostly on details, and sometimes fail to see the bigger picture. If they do succeed in discerning a totality, it is because they see the sum of added-up details. Furthermore, it proves extremely difficult for them to take the context into consideration.

We believe this autistic way of thinking – experiencing their world in detail – is the base of everything that makes people with autism different from others. As a consequence, we notice it in the way they act, think, socialise, communicate and relate to others. We like to use the iceberg analogy. The biggest part, which is hidden under water and cannot be seen, represents the autistic way of thinking. Everything above the water in plain sight represents their utterances and is the result of this way of thinking – everything in the behaviour and thinking of autistic people that we tend to think of as different from what we regard as 'normal'.

Because of the fact that this focus on detail is so basic to people with autism and so fundamentally different from the way non-autistic people perceive reality, we believe it to be crucial to see people with autism as being different.

In addition to this, we find it very important, and essential in our way of working, that we do not approach their problems by treating them as deficient or as having shortcomings. Their autism does leave them with certain limitations, but on the other hand it provides strengths and opportunities. What matters is that we discern these qualities.

Despite this vision, we are not blind to the limitations and problems people with autism struggle with in our society. It is absolutely important for a professional worker to have a clear idea of the exact nature of these limitations. This is what Part II is about.

AUTISTIC THINKING AS ANOTHER CULTURE

Because people with autism perceive the world in a completely different way, they give other meanings to what they see and experience. As a result, they will behave in ways that might seem 'weird' or strange to us. The connection between perception of reality, giving meaning and following behaviour can be pictured as in Figure 1.2.[1]

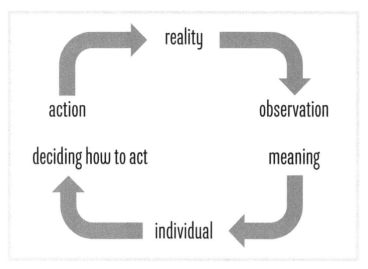

Figure 1.2   Coherence

People perceive reality with all of their senses. While observing reality, the brain processes sensory stimuli. This process results in the giving of a meaning. Depending on our personality, history, context, previous experiences, values, ideas, etc. we give a certain meaning to certain stimuli or events. Based on our own thoughts, habits, experiences, etc., we assign meaning, and consequently opt for a specific action. Finally, we perform this action. This implies that meaning results in a certain choice of action, and thus in effective behaviour.

The reaction to these actions and their effect has in its turn an influence on the meaning we assign. It is a circular process in which thinking and acting have a never-ending mutual effect on each other. We see now that this process does not work in the same way with people with autism, but has a particular fashion of its own.

First of all, they experience and process sensory stimuli in a different way.[2] In addition to the five external senses, there are two internal senses: a sense of equilibrium and proprioception (sense of position). The organs of balance detect rotating movements of the body in every direction. Because of that, they have a significant effect on our sense of balance and movement. The sensory cells responsible for our sense of position inform us about our posture and the movements every part of our body makes. Scientists have discovered that people with autism tend to react either over-sensitively or under-sensitively to some of these sensory stimuli.

J. always wears a backpack in which she keeps her sunglasses and her earplugs. She struggles with sunlight: it gives her headaches. Fluorescent light is unbearable to her. In places with a lot of noise, she feels compelled to use her earplugs. If she doesn't, she gets overstimulated very quickly, and this results in physical pain. This overstimulation makes it necessary for her to leave. On the other hand, she fails to notice when she's hungry (proprioception). She has learned to eat at fixed times. She doesn't recognise the feeling of 'hunger'.

C. is a 45-year-old woman. She knows how to drive a car and visits our therapeutic centre on her own. The road leads by a canal, which is lined with trees. Sunlight flashes through these trees when she passes them. That makes it very hard for her to drive that road. The sudden flashes are so intense for her that she has to stop halfway to calm herself down.

During training courses I like to use a projector for my presentations. Whenever M. accompanies me to speak from his experience, he cannot begin talking as long as the projector is working. That is because the machine produces a monotonous buzz, and M. is not able to ignore that noise.

J. is a very gifted man with autism. He cannot feel warmth, nor cold. As a result, he goes out on his bike in the middle of winter with nothing but a t-shirt on.

E. is an intelligent woman with autism, a teacher. She complains about headaches, especially in the evenings. After an exploratory conversation, it turns out that E. does not feel thirst. She forgets to drink during the day, and that causes her headaches. She concludes that she should drink a glass of water every time she takes a break. It turns out her headaches are as good as gone after that. But she now notices that she gets bad-tempered every Sunday, around eleven o'clock. She has no clue whatsoever why. Experience had taught me that people with autism often don't feel hunger. She ponders this for a while, and decides to grab a bite halfway through the morning. It makes her mood a lot better on Sundays.

Olga Bogdashina states that there are many indications that autistic persons often have trouble dissociating sensory stimuli in the foreground from those in the background.[3] They take them all in with the same amount of detail. Moreover, they experience each separate piece of information as a unit in itself. For them, a scene consists of a whole lot of separate particles that add up into that one scene. When one of those particles changes, the whole scene will be different.

A boy with autism goes on a school trip for the first time, and cannot use the toilet. It turns out that the toilet seats in the place they stay are old-fashioned black ones.

But the boy only knows toilets with white seats. If it has a black seat, it is not a toilet to him...

Moreover, it became apparent that if there is too much information that needs to be processed simultaneously, people with autism are unable to divide that information into small meaningful pieces.

K. tells me that as a child he found it very difficult to recognise his class with his classmates each time somebody switched places. The classroom he knew consisted of that very room, with these same people on their fixed spots on the room. If places were traded, he considered it another class.

This example illustrates that people with autism give a different meaning to experiences, a meaning that people without autism often cannot understand. Therefore, people with autism respond to these experiences in a way that is likely to be found 'weird' or unusual by other people. But if you take the time to learn how people with autism give meaning to experiences, it turns out that their actions aren't illogical at all.

They are just different.

We can compare this to people from different cultures. For example, if Greek people throw their heads backwards and simultaneously click their tongues very subtly, that means 'no'. They move their heads sideways to indicate a 'yes'. If you don't know this when talking to a Greek person, there could definitely be a lot of confusion and misunderstanding.

If we have a conversation with somebody from a different culture, we are very much aware that they give different meanings to things. We ask for explanations, we make issues concrete to understand them better, and we adapt our own behaviour.

In the same way, if one wants to cooperate with somebody with autism, it is of the utmost importance that one gives enough thought to possible meanings they might attribute to experiences, stimuli and events.

AUTISTIC PEOPLE AND THE SOLUTION-FOCUSED APPROACH: A PERFECT MATCH

We try to maintain this basic attitude at all times, and with all of our clients. We approach our clients with an attitude of 'not knowing': we, the professionals, are not the ones who know what is best for them. Of course, we can make suggestions, but in the end it will be our clients who decide what they will or won't do, or how they will lead their lives. This basic attitude is fundamental in a solution-focused approach: the client is his or her own life's best expert.

A solution-focused professional carefully explores their client's frames of reference. We accept the way the client perceives the world. We try to find perceptions that can help the client to achieve a greater feeling of wellbeing (similar to the difference between calling a glass half full or half empty). Sometimes we suggest another point of view that provides our client with more options as to how he or she thinks or acts.[4]

An attitude of 'not knowing' is essential. This attitude implies that professionals listen to their clients with genuine curiosity.[5] They get behind their clients, and look with them in the same direction, towards their goal.

Different culture, different motivation

In a solution-focused approach the goals of the client are pivotal. The professional will try to define, together with the client, the goals that are specific to them. What is their motivation? Which goal is so important that the client is willing to undertake action to reach it?

The dictionary defines motivation as 'to be prepared to carry out certain behaviour'. People approach a therapist because there is an occasion, a need or a demand for help. That demand for help can come from themselves, from their immediate surroundings (parents, partner, family) or from another authority that pushes them to go to therapy.

Every therapist wants their assistance to be useful for the client. Eventually the purpose of therapy is to help clients, and to help them move forward. People perceive something as useful when it coincides with their own goals, with what motivates them. If a goal is defined clearly, the therapist as well as the client knows very well where the therapy leads to and when the goal is achieved.

Over the years, we have noticed that the motivation for a person with autism is on the one hand similar to that of a person without autism, but that on the other it differs fundamentally. That is why we like to elaborate on this subject. Professional workers see motivation very often as the key to change.

In scientific literature a distinction is made between two sorts of motivation: intrinsic motivation and extrinsic motivation.

Intrinsic motivation
This is the sort of motivation people hold within themselves: their ambitions, their interests or the satisfaction they get from an achievement.

Extrinsic motivation

This is the sort of motivation people get from performing an act that comes with a reward: a diploma, an amount of money or any other material or immaterial compensation, for example, status or family honour. Extrinsic motivation can be very strong, especially if certain behaviour is rewarded with social appreciation. For example, you perform an act that yields applause, admiration, a better relationship, compliments or even love – this can be extremely motivating.

Bestowing strong social reward to desired behaviour can cause a change in attitude, especially with children. However, people with autism are often not as sensitive to social rewards. Yet people expect them to behave in a certain way that is prescribed by social habits. When that happens, the non-autistic person will often try and explain, with not a little frustration, why they expect the person with autism to behave in such a way. In fact, we expect everybody to behave or function with appreciation of the social reward.

For example, at a very early age, children learn to greet certain people with a handshake, others with a kiss. It all depends on who it is you're greeting. A child without autism grabs this idea fairly quickly. We often see that young children will kiss everybody they meet, but they don't do this for long. The reaction of their parents or other important people soon makes clear what is expected of them. This doesn't work for a child with autism. Many people with autism find it hard to give someone a kiss. It's too close to be comfortable, it's wet and unpleasant. Because of these sensory issues, they do not feel any intrinsic motivation at all. Quite the opposite, in fact.

Moreover, they don't understand why this could be important. What's the use? Why do people find it important? The purpose of these actions is very hard to explain in a concrete way. They are based on social agreements that have been around for ages. People with autism understand things best when they are concrete. All things social are less concrete. In other words, we often ask a person with autism to do something that they regard as completely useless.

A lot of people with autism are not very motivated by social rewards. How can you motivate someone to do something they find useless? In this case, it can be useful to try and find something intrinsic or a particular extrinsic motivation that may be important to this person, to achieve the desired behaviour.

Our experience is that it is very hard to motivate people with autism to do something that they believe to be useless. Because they have another view of the world, another frame of reference, the extrinsic rewards we commonly use are unmotivating for them. We need to find an extrinsic motivator and make it as concrete as possible.

> S. is a 21-year-old man with autism. He works for a company building stages and theatrical scenes. It's hard work: parts of stages and scaffolding are heavy. When he comes home he never takes a shower. The only time he does is on Saturday evening before he goes out. His mother is annoyed by his smell when he sits down to eat. He, on the other hand, does not mind his smell. His mother has tried to explain to him why she wants him to take a shower more often. But it didn't work. Together we went on a search for ways that might motivate him. We decided to try this: I visit them once a month. And every

time I do, I ask his mother whether he has taken a weekly shower. Each time he showered in the middle of the week, I give him 50 cents. It worked well. Obtaining money, even in small amounts, motivated him enough to make an effort to wash.

DETAILED THINKING: IMPLICATIONS

The autistic way of thinking, or detailed thinking, has a lot of implications for people with autism. In scientific literature, writers use the term 'the triad'[6] to refer to everything that distinguishes or indicates autism. The triad entails their difference in communicating, social relationships and way of thinking and acting.

We see several results in different domains of living that all come down to the same baseline: the underlying detailed thinking and the different way of processing and experiencing sensory clues.

Being different in communication
Implications for the understanding of language

Communicating is all about exchanging information or meanings. Very often, what is said is not what is meant. Just think of the use of irony, hidden meanings or emotions, and humour.

There is a functional and a relational level to communication. The functional part of communication works fine with people with autism, but the relational part tends to cause problems. The first meaning they hear is a literal one, as you probably noticed in our previous examples. Growing older, most people with autism learn that a great deal of communication is not to be interpreted literally. Still, it always takes time for them to think beyond what is literally there. And sometimes they fail.

We have sometimes experienced a long latency between asking a question and getting the answer. People need time to decode the question, formulate an answer and then encode that answer into a language that the other party understands. Conversations with someone with autism tend to have fewer topics. Knowing the first meaning they hear is a literal one, one can understand that many people with autism find it hard to understand abstract words, sayings, humour or proverbs.

> I used to work with young kids in a revalidation centre [a centre where children can get logotherapy, psychomotoric therapy, psychotherapy, etc.]. Together with a colleague I trained them in social cognition. One of the first days – I was not that familiar with autism yet – I asked S. 'Can you sit on that chair?' She said yes, and remained standing.

> During one of the exercises we asked one of the kids 'to go outside'. G. got scared. 'Do I need to go outside? It is dark outside!' Of course, what we meant was that G. was to go and stand in the hallway.

> D. had learned the saying 'night falls'. That night he was very afraid when it turned dark. He thought the night would literally fall on his head.

Consequences for the use of language

As a consequence of detailed thinking, people with autism generally have a different (and for us more limited) communicative mindset. That means for them it isn't obvious to know what it is they have to communicate.

People without autism are 'specialists' in asking open questions. But a conversation partner with autism often doesn't know how to answer such questions: What is it you want to know? What are you really asking for?

The question 'What did you do today?' can refer to a lot of things. Somebody with autism will struggle to understand the goal of the question and the intentions of the person asking it. Does he or she want to know:

» What I ate?

» Which clothes I wore?

» Who was with me?

» If the weather was fine?

» What was the colour of the boots I wore?

» Where I went?

Depending on who's talking, other answers are expected. Generally, you'd share different things with your boss than you would with a friend. You'd be more concise, less personal in your answer. People without autism have an instinct for that. For people with autism, this seems to be more of an effort.

> M. says he finds it very hard to answer if a neighbour asks him how he is. He knows social protocol prescribes him to simply answer 'fine'. But if he doesn't feel that well at all, he likes to say so. 'Fine' is not right in this context. Yet he always tries to give an answer that is as concise as he can.

Consequences in conversation

During a conversation, there is a constant swap of roles. Addressor becomes addressee and vice versa.

One moment you talk while the other listens, the next you listen to them. This roleplay is hard for people with autism. And indeed, it is a complicated play, when you consider it: you must understand what the other is saying or asking, then you have to reply, and then they say something else...and for someone without autism this doesn't take any effort at all. It happens, in fact, without any thinking.

For people with autism, this process is extremely challenging. Having a conversation with two or three people is hard enough, but following a conversation in a larger group is almost impossible. That is because their different way of thinking makes it hard for them to keep an overview. In a 'normal' conversation a large variety of topics passes by. Therefore one needs a very flexible mindset to follow and engage in this conversation and that is a problem for people with autism. They lose sight of the overview, and their attention slips away.

> T. tells us that he cannot participate in conversations with three persons or more. It takes a while before he realises what the others are talking about. Then he needs time to think of what he could add to the subject. And when he finally does find something to say, the subject has already changed...

Being different in social interaction

An additional consequence of autistic thinking turns up in social interactions between people with and people without autism. We notice some differences in quality during their communication.

First of all, there is a difference in non-verbal interaction. People with autism tend to use very little body language. A lot of them do not support their communication with gestures at all. They notice the non-verbal communication of others, but are not always able to give meaning to it. Even for people without autism, it is not always easy to understand non-verbal communication or to interpret non-verbal communication in the right way.

But, as it turns out, even more than others, people with autism find it very difficult to attribute the right meaning to someone's bodily communication. People without autism are accustomed to certain reactions that may be triggered by their non-verbal communication. For example, when someone starts to cry individuals with autism often don't know how to react.

> S. is a 40-year-old man with autism. He has a girlfriend. He told her a couple of times that he would like her to be very specific about what she expects him to do when, for instance, she cries or gets angry. If she doesn't tell him literally, he cannot know what it is she needs at that moment.

Because they experience social interaction in a different way, there are also differences in their ability to engage in a relationship. Many autistic people find it hard to connect with their peers. Although they may succeed in making an acquaintance, engaging in a real and long-lasting friendship requires some effort. We are expected to remember important issues, to get in touch regularly, to go out on dates and have fun together, to list just a few expectations.

This aspect of social relations can be extremely challenging for people with autism. It is not in their nature to propose spontaneously doing something together, to give a call without a specific reason, etc. However, this does not imply that they have no need for social contact.

Often what is most remarkable about engaging in a relationship with someone with autism is the lack of social-emotional reciprocity. A 'normal' conversation, with a back-and-forth rhythm, rarely occurs. People with autism are unable to discern or imagine what another person thinks, would like or expects. They also lack the flexibility to fluently react to what the other says or does.

It also seems as if autistic people don't share a lot about themselves spontaneously. This sort of sharing is foundational to a conversation or a relationship. People generally talk about what they like, what they're involved in; they talk about themselves. Yet when individuals with autism do this, it might be inappropriate. They focus mostly on their own interests and activities, and fail to include those of the other. In this way, communication often result in a one-way monologue.

During our therapy sessions I sometimes talk about my own life, about my children for instance. Someone with autism often doesn't react to such information. All they do is register what I am saying without further comment.

Being different in ways of thinking and behaving

Finally, we discern differences in behaviour and interest. We notice differences in behaviour because many people with autism have a stereotypical way of acting. These actions can be either verbal or behavioural tics. Some people scratch themselves when feeling uncomfortable, others make certain recurring movements with their hands, while others have facial tics.

As for verbal behaviour, we notice, for instance, (postponed) echolalia, which means they literally repeat what somebody else has said. Some individuals with autism repeat certain combinations of words, always in the same order.

> When I met M.'s parents, it turned out that a lot of what M. said, she had heard literally from her mother: she used the same intonation, the same words, the same sentences.

In addition, people with autism have fixed routines and rituals. These are series of actions that are acted out in a fixed sequence. People without autism have routines as well; routines or habits make life easier. These differ from autistic routines, though, because they are variable. Somebody with autism isn't able to adapt their routines easily to a changing situation.

> J. can only brush her teeth when she's wearing her nightgown. If she is already dressed, she cannot brush her teeth.

> D. gets up in the morning, drinks a cup of coffee and turns on the computer. He plays for a couple of hours and then dresses himself. When he has an early appointment, he needs to prepare in advance. Or he gets up a lot earlier so he can still go through his usual routine.

When it comes to interests, most people with autism are rather limited. Although their interests can change in the course of time, they tend to be quite static, and consume much of their spare time. A person with autism feels a strong need, an urge in fact, to be occupied with their subject of interest. It is almost impossible for them to spend their spare time in any other way, without help from others.

T. is a 16-year-old boy. When he gets home, he hurries through his homework, so he can go and play a videogame as quickly as possible. In his spare time, the only thing he does is play that same game over and over again. Getting better at it makes him feel good. But when there's an evening he cannot play, he feels uncomfortable. He doesn't know how to spend his spare time in another way.

Finally, we discern preoccupation with parts of subjects. This comes down to what we think of as the essence of autism, that is, autistic thinking or thinking in details. When you focus on details, it is hard to assess the context.

When talking to autistic people, we need to be aware at all times of this autistic way of thinking. We tend to take it for granted that people know how to generalise solutions, explanations and other verbal messages, and that people are consequently able to recognise similar situations. This is an ability that people with autism do not have. No situation is identical to another.

This way of thinking results in a limited imagination. When somebody tries to imagine something, they generally begin with an overview: where, who, what, how. People with autism find it very difficult to make such an overview, because of their trouble with assessing contexts.

SOLUTION-FOCUSED DIAGNOSIS

In this book we focus on people with a diagnosis of autism. People with autism have often experienced difficulties in different areas of their life for many years. They notice that they see some things differently. This frequently causes high levels of tension and anxiety as well as constant stress, which can lead to decompensation (such as depression, illness or psychosis). These secondary concerns often precipitate a longing for an explanation for their 'being different'. This results in a request for testing, for diagnostic examination. In most cases, people don't ask for a diagnosis without an incentive. Furthermore, they mostly tell us that the feeling of being fundamentally different from others has always been there. By performing several tests and observations during the diagnostic process, we notice that the person with autism looks at the world in a very detail-focused way. They do not take into account the context, nor do they connect details into a coherent unity.

The official criteria by which autism is diagnosed are determined by the DSM.

THE USEFULNESS OF AUTISM DIAGNOSIS

A diagnostician generally enumerates everything that isn't working. By definition, the focus here is on the client's limitations and what is wrong. The DSM-5 is recognised officially by diagnosticians as the manual of psychiatric problems. As such, the DSM uses a language that is very much problem-oriented. It is an enumeration of problems and limitations.

We have pointed out why a lot of our patients turn to diagnostic examination. When this examination confirms that the client does have an autistic way of thinking, it is often met with dismay, even if it does help them to recognise what is happening. Sometimes, however, there is a sense of relief.

Because it is very difficult to assess the gravity of the limitations of people with autism and precisely because a test results in a long list of limitations, we find it very important to evaluate beforehand whether an (official) diagnosis is really necessary or useful.

That is why, as professionals, we think it is very important to search for the motives that lie behind the request for a test or diagnostic examination. Yet again, it is fundamental to adopt an attitude of 'not knowing' when listening to the client's questions. As professional mental health workers, we believe it is our duty to ask a few fundamental questions in advance:

» Is a diagnosis useful for this client?

» Is diagnosis useful for the people surrounding the client?

» Is diagnosis in the long run useful for the client's personal development and wellbeing?

» What are the possible advantages and downsides of diagnosis for this client?

Each of these questions should be addressed in a conversation.

Is a diagnosis useful for this client?

Experience has taught us that people with autism who have a normal intellectual capacity realise they are different, in most cases. To have a label put on their being different comes as a relief to most of them, because it provides a framework in which a lot of the difficulties they have experienced can be understood. The disability is still there, but it becomes more manageable when people know the thinking mechanisms that lie beneath it. The person with autism can get a sharper view of who they are. Furthermore, many difficulties develop new meaning. For many people with autism this new insight helps to diminish guilty feelings.

> E. is a 32-year-old woman. Her son has been diagnosed with autism, and as a result she decides to have herself tested as well. When she too is diagnosed with autism, this comes to her as a relief: 'I always knew I was different. I always try as hard as I can to do what I suppose is expected of me, but I fail a lot. Now I know it is not my fault, it's not because I'm lazy. I don't always understand you, because I think differently.'

On the other hand, the autism label can be frightening. The medical world and society regard those with autism as being disabled. In most cases they fail to see opportunities, coping mechanisms, strengths or talents.

In our experience, people with autism are sometimes disregarded. Yet with a little effort to understand the way of thinking of a person with autism, one will discover strong coping mechanisms. Because these are often not recognised, autistic people tend to have a feeling of being restricted, and rightfully so.

If we feel that making a diagnosis is not useful for a particular client, we will advise against diagnostic examination. Sometimes, we as therapists already know that the client will most probably be diagnosed with autism, but there is no added value to have a diagnosis: not for the client, nor their surroundings, nor for us as therapists. If such is the case, we proceed without diagnosis. Moreover, there is no need for a diagnosis for us to proceed with our work in a solution-focused way. A person can make progress in many ways. Because solution-focused thinking is based on the self-healing forces of a person, on his or her talents, resources and possibilities, diagnosis is not compulsory.

The therapeutic hypothesis of autism can be useful knowledge for the therapist though, even if he or she doesn't share it with the client. A hypothesis such as this can cause the therapist or professional helper to adapt their speech or approach, and to be aware of possible restrictions.

Is diagnosis useful for the people surrounding the client?

Very often we notice that, in particular, the people close to a client find peace in a diagnosis. Parents, partners and others experience the person with autism as someone who is difficult to live with. He or she seems to have a specific manual that he operates by. When a diagnosis is made, the proximal processes (those family and friends closest to the individual) can link the difficulties they experience to the different way of thinking of the person involved. This offers new possibilities, new ways of approaching and adapting. It creates new resources and opportunities to help. Moreover, a diagnosis can help to alleviate the guilt that is often experienced in those proximal processes. It provides them too with a framework that helps them to understand why things are so difficult or different.

When it comes to society, the diagnosis of autism spectrum disorder can be useful in that it may provide access to much needed external resources. In Belgium and Flanders (the northern part of Belgium), it enables you to make use of several levels of customised social work, such as assisted living, inclusive education, access to day care centres, specialised job-coaching or any form of adapted employment. Bear in mind, though, that not everybody with autism is in need of such assistance.

Is diagnosis in the long run useful for the client's personal development and wellbeing?

A better understanding of oneself can result in a feeling of more control over situations in which you may find yourself. This is the same for all people – with or without autism. When people with autism are, through diagnosis, able to make contact with peers and professionals and learn how to connect more easily with people in their surroundings, this often leads to a greater sense of wellbeing. If this diagnosis creates a better understanding of the way in which they are different, and if it helps the people around them to find a more adequate way to interact with them, it goes without saying that this will make everybody involved feel better.

A (solution-focused) professional worker can operate as a catalyst. Indeed, the goal of a therapeutic process is to create a context in which the client (and their proximal processes) can reflect on different meanings, different solutions, on what is already working. In this way, you can steadily search for ways to improve the situation by restoring, developing or expanding possibilities.

What are the possible advantages and downsides of diagnosis for this client?

Of course, this question relates to the previous ones. A lot depends on the specific kind of help the client has asked for, on the context in which he or she functions, on the nature of the difficulties. Zooming in on possible pros and cons is very much a hypothetical issue. We can never take all aspects of life into consideration. But discussing opportunities and restrictions of diagnosis creates options for the client and their proximal processes.

WHAT HAPPENS AFTER DIAGNOSIS?

A diagnosis confronts its subject with many restrictions. People are told that the disorder is pervasive, and that it is a disorder that affects all aspects of life and wellbeing. That is why after a diagnosis we often see that people go through a period of grieving. To be brought face to face with such limitations and their consequences, and to integrate these into our lives, requires hard work and takes time. Like all mourning processes, it fluctuates. There will be days of faith and belief in the diagnosis; there will be days of anger and sadness; there will also be days of disbelief. The homeostatic balance of a person and their system are disturbed.

Previous experiences have shown that some people seem to behave in an even more autistic manner after their diagnosis. They let go of some of their intensive coping mechanisms in order to gain enough energy to deal with the mourning process. After a while, the person with autism, together with their family and friends, usually find a new equilibrium in which opportunities and limitations can coexist.

After people with autism have learned about the limitations that come with their diagnosis, the therapist is challenged to put these limitations into perspective. After all, these people have overcome many challenges and difficulties without the diagnosis. It is our task to focus on the elements that helped them build up their lives until now, and to enhance these elements. A solution-focused therapist believes that every human being, despite or due to their limitations, has untapped possibilities and resources. The therapist searches for those possibilities and makes them clear and visible.

However, a solution-focused approach does not imply that the therapist tries to avoid discussing difficulties or problems. Recognising these problems is especially crucial for the therapy. Clients want and need to feel heard and understood.

In the solution-focused framework we distinguish between two categories of 'difficulties'.[7] On the one hand, there are 'limitations'. These are the difficulties for which we cannot find temporary or lasting solutions. These limitations can be the consequence of a disorder, a disease or choices that have been made. A limitation prevents us from making certain choices: it deprives us from options because there are no solutions, and there is no way around a limitation. In that way, everything that has happened in the past is by definition a limitation.

I have two children. The options I have are constrained by that reality. For instance, I cannot go travelling unexpectedly.

On the other hand, there are difficulties for which we can now, or in the near future, find solutions. We refer to these difficulties as 'problems'.

This distinction is very useful when considering people with autism. It challenges us to look for solutions in a creative way, and within the right context.

Autism as such is not always a limitation. If somebody with autism lives and functions in an environment that is suitable for them, that is, adapted to their wishes or needs, autism will be less of a limitation. If, on the other hand, a person with autism must engage in complex social situations, if the environment has expectations they cannot live up to due to their autism, this will cause problems.

We cannot find a solution for autism, as such – we cannot remove the autism. But we are able to help and think of possible solutions that will facilitate living with the consequences of autism.

H. is a young lady with autism who has a lot of difficulties with changes. To move over from one task to another is very hard for her. As a teacher she finds it very stressful to change classes all the time. The restriction is difficulties with transitions. We cannot make this go away.

The problem here can be described as being stressed when transitioning to different classes.

Together we explored ways to deal with this problem. We looked at what was helping in other moments that got her stressed. And it turned out that, in other stressful situations, performing a little ritual helped her remain calm. A ritual she used at home to move on from one chore to the next was to drink a glass of water. She concluded herself that this was something she could do in school as well. She decided to drink half a glass of water after every class. This resulted in making the transition a lot easier for her.

Some problems can be seen as 'abilities not yet acquired'.[8] During their lives, people develop new skills all the time. Some of these are achieved in organic ways, others must be learned.

N., a young woman with autism, presented me with this problem: she wanted to apply for college, but first she needed to engage in a motivational conversation as part of the admission requirements. She really wanted to do her very best and was very nervous about it, because she couldn't imagine what kind of questions she would be asked. Furthermore, she didn't know how to respond in a good way, how to behave, what body language to use, etc.

This problem can be translated to an ability not yet acquired: the ability to participate in an application interview.

Together we thought of possible questions, and we performed a roleplay in which she learned how to enter the room, say hello, answer the questions and say goodbye. Body language turned out to be the biggest problem for her. We zoomed in on different types of body language, so she could find out for herself which type suited best for the occasion. Later she told me that she had followed the scenario we had made together, and that she was accepted.

Gifted people with autism have unconsciously, throughout their lives, assembled a large range of coping mechanisms. It is a therapist's goal to explore and explain these mechanisms together with the client, in order for them to gain conscious control over these skills, and thus gain better control over their lives.

At the same time, people with autism often experience feeling misunderstood and yet they have coped with that one way or another. Experience teaches that most people first and foremost need to feel understood and that they are being listened to. It is not easy to live with autism in a society that sets high standards on communication, social skills and flexibility. Autism restricts our clients, and those who seek help often like to hear that they – despite their restrictions – have been doing a very good job.

Throughout their lives, autistic people are frequently told that they are weird, do things that don't fit, act in inappropriate ways, that they should respond differently and that they don't live up to a lot of societal expectations (having a lot of friends, a busy social life, hobbies, etc.).

We have learned that our clients have seen quite a few social assistants and therapists. Sometimes they found someone who helped them; many times, though, they only faced incomprehension. The fact that they have the courage to see someone new yet again is so admirable. We try and recognise this when people finally decide to come and see us. We regard that kind of courage as a nice gift to the helper, as it bears witness to a lot of effort and a strong will to understand oneself and others.

In the second part of this book, we will make a number of suggestions on how to use this gift in a useful way.

PART II

PRACTICE

3

ADAPTING THE THERAPEUTIC CONTEXT TO A DIFFERENT CULTURE

From our basic view, seeing autism as a fundamentally different way of being in the world, the concept 'D.I.F.F.E.R.E.N.T.' was born. Our target – to offer a solution-focused manual for working with people with autism – has already been reached to a considerable extent if we succeed in helping professional workers and others involved to share this perspective. If we approach people with autism with the basic attitude of respect, 'not knowing', listening and asking questions, equality, understanding and empathy, we think that we have done a very good job.

It is our experience that having both a good understanding of what autism is, and a solution-focused approach is the key to success. We were (and are) often asked whether working in a solution-focused way with people with autism is even possible at all. We are very much convinced it is, provided solution-focused techniques and questions are adapted to the autistic way of thinking. Based on our experiences of what is working, we edited a practical manual.

Having a conversation with people with autism is different from talking to neurotypical (non-autistic) people. These conversations are different because of the autistic way of thinking, which requires that we take into account a number of specific particularities.

Communication requires insight in action–reaction. It is expected that both speaking partners can start and maintain a conversation, that they understand what the other is saying, etc. But these communication tasks are very difficult for people with autism. Yet it is possible, through some adaptations by the therapist, to build a rapport that feels satisfying for the client.

Regardless of the therapeutic framework from which you assist people, the following aspects are of great importance in order to have a fruitful conversation with somebody with autism.

RULE 1: TAKE INTO ACCOUNT THE DIFFERENT WAY OF COMMUNICATING AND ADAPT YOUR STYLE

When we zoom in on the way in which we communicate with others, we see that people are inclined to say things in a very indirect way. We tend to go from Bruges to Brussels via Paris, so to speak. In an attempt not to hurt the other's feelings, to please the other and at the same time to show them how we see reality, we often hide second meanings behind concrete words.

> A woman says to her husband, 'Baby, that ring over there, I like that one very much...', and she gives him her sweetest smile. What she actually means is: 'Buy that ring for me.'

A person with autism will always first interpret something literally. They understand the words as they are said, and do not take the context or underlying meanings into account. Many people with autism, however, especially those at the high-functioning end of the spectrum, have learned that people often mean more than what they literally say. They are very alert to this and try very hard to decipher the actual meaning. Sometimes it works, but often it doesn't, or it takes them a lot of time to decipher the intended meaning. Imagine that every time your partner says something, you have to stop and think about what he or she wants to say. How tiresome would that be?

That is why it is of the utmost importance that we make use of a very concrete and clear language in a therapeutic setting, whether it be verbal or non-verbal. Say what you mean, be transparent. Short and clear questions are best understood by people with autism. It is also desirable for a therapist to take their client's restricted imagination into account. So: the more concrete, the better.

> F. told me this a couple of times: if somebody asks him a question, he repeats that question for himself in his mind. He tries to find out what the other wants to know (decoding). The next step is to formulate an answer in his mind (coding). And only then does he express that answer out loud.

This example has been confirmed by many clients. Concretely this means that the latency between question and answer is long. We should give the person involved the time he or she needs to think of an answer. In a conversation with somebody with autism a lot less is said compared to when we talk to somebody without autism. As a result, a slow pace is required in order to communicate with somebody with autism in a qualitative way.

RULE 2: VISUALISE

The same words can have a completely different meaning for different people, and that makes it very hard for people with autism. Truly, we are not as objective as we might think when it comes to our language. Add to that the fact that people with autism find it difficult to hold on to spoken words: they tend to think more in images.

A therapist will always try to connect with their client. In order to do so, they will try and speak the same language. Based on the assumption that our target group understands visual language more easily, it is necessary to support your spoken language as much as possible with images. In a practical way visualising means: make language visible, turn it into images. An image or drawing never changes and therefore leaves nothing to the imagination.

That is not an easy task. It turns out that there are different ways to do this. Every person is different, so each time, we have to search for what fits this person best. Mostly we use a notebook, in which we write short key words, social scripts and conclusions. Apart from that, we make a lot of drawings to support or clarify things that are being said. There is no need for those drawings to be nice or beautiful, complicated or even realistic. It is sufficient if both parties understand what it is about. We give the notebook to our client so they can take it home and review and rethink everything that has been said. They can also use it as a guide to tell somebody else about our conversation and what it was about. And finally, we encourage our client to write things down: questions, goals or thoughts they had in between our meetings.

For some people with autism, speaking in metaphors works really well. It is very important, though, to choose metaphors that relate closely to the client's frame of reference. If you're talking to somebody who loves to work with computers, make use of metaphors related to computers. Metaphors often clarify what you really mean. These metaphors grow even stronger when you support them with non-verbal language.

The process of action and reaction in a system often recurs in a conversation. I like to compare this to a game of tennis: if one hits the ball and the other just hits back, the game will last endlessly. If you want the other to do something, if you want to provoke him or her, you hit the ball harder, softer, sideways, etc. I often support this with the drawing in Figure 3.1.

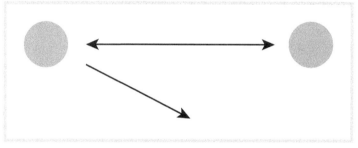

Figure 3.1   Action–reaction

RULE 3: TAKE INTO ACCOUNT THE DIFFERENT WAY OF PROCESSING INFORMATION, AND MAKE SURE THAT THE INFORMATION IS ORGANISED IN ADVANCE

Experience shows that people with autism tend to tell stories in a very chaotic way: the autistic brain does not discern principal or less important matters; everything is equally important. Add to that the fact that people with autism are often very good at making associations. This makes their story even less coherent. Some therapists therefore choose to set an agenda in advance, so it is clear what the conversation will be about.

It is the therapist's task to listen really well, to make possible links in time and space, and to ask for clarifications. The therapist is responsible for the kinds of question he or she asks, and for the clarification of contexts.

In solution-focused, conversational therapy, it is the client who defines the content. The therapist determines the nature of the process. In a setting such as this, the therapist doesn't set an agenda beforehand. The therapist allows the client to guide the conversation. Many clients find it useful to prepare what they really want to discuss. In that way, the therapist puts all responsibility for the content of the conversation with the client.

RULE 4: KEEP PSYCHO-EDUCATION AS HOPEFUL AS POSSIBLE

Psycho/social education is an essential part of assistance for people with autism. It concerns specific psycho-educational aspects of autism – the autistic way of thinking and its consequences. It is about how the client acts and possible reactions from others, and about social interaction with others.

Because of their autistic thinking, people with autism don't understand a lot about themselves and their environment. Psycho/social education helps these people to better understand some issues, to put them in a referential framework and to find possibilities to deal with them in a different way.

A lot of books are written on this subject. Most of them concentrate on the restrictions, or the term 'disabled'. We, on the other hand, very consciously choose to teach psycho/social education in a much more hopeful way. It is a fact that autism causes some restrictions. But this doesn't mean that those restrictions are always present. In some situations, thinking differently can even be an advantage.

From the moment people receive their diagnosis, it is clear that autism is a condition that won't go away. However, it is absolutely not a static issue. People change during their lives. Development assumes that an individual learns new things. Every day we experience things that trigger minor adaptations so that we see or do things just a little differently, or understand them better. The same goes for people with autism.

In psycho/social education about autism and autistic thinking, good dosage is of the utmost importance. Most of the time people are in need of an explanation of what is happening right now, of what they are doing at this moment. It is not useful to give abundant theory. And it is important to go slow.

As we said before, we make a distinction between problems and restrictions. If people get a better insight to what a problem is, and what a restriction is, expectations become more realistic. People with autism are eager to learn how to deal in a better way with the restrictions their 'being different' imposes. The goal of assistance is often to offer tools to lessen the consequences of those restrictions (problems).

When teaching psycho/social education it is extremely useful to listen to your client very closely. Listening in this context means therapists should question their clients thoroughly about how they experience certain situations, and which explanation is most needed at this particular moment. The more concrete a situation becomes to you and your client, the more precisely you can tune your explanation to his or her needs or questions.

As a result, a professional helper needs to first ask themselves, and then the client (since the client is the only one who holds the answers) questions such as the following:

» What is concretely happening?

» What are they (already) doing?

» What is somebody else doing?

» Where is it happening?

Narratives

When teaching our clients with autism psycho/social education about autism, we like to use narratives. By 'narratives' we mean stories about the way things go in the life of others. We tell stories about how other people think, how they live, what they expect, etc. In line with the narratives Erickson used in his hypnotherapy,[9] we believe (and experience daily) that stories can enhance some of the client's emotions, behaviour or cognitions.

By using anecdotes, we can make suggestions to do things in a different way or not, or to change one's view on something. When using such a story it is very important that the client can identify with what is told. This implies that the therapist has to listen very carefully to what the client is saying, and also that the story relates to the client's interests and environment.

We tell our client: 'Another client, who has autism as well, has found a solution for that. Every time he or she..., he or she does this...and that helps. Might that be something that would work for you as well?'

Narratives can be used to highlight specific resources for the client. Such a resource is something that proves useful to reach a certain goal. Everyone holds some of these resources in themselves: in a detail of character, certain skills or talents, etc. At the same time, there are external resources (people, situations, contexts) that can help to reach a specific goal. Using narratives can bring forward certain inner strengths of the client or strengths in their environment, so he or she is able to see them. Finally, we can use narratives to normalise and to explain.[10]

We have noticed that, for some people, the use of stories works even better when you don't look at them while you recount the narrative. In that way, the client doesn't have to take non-verbal behaviour into account. They can concentrate fully on the contents of the story.

Social Stories™

Social Stories[11] are similar instruments. Social Stories differ from narratives in that they focus on the social interactions between several persons in a social context. Our clients sometimes wonder how they should behave in a specific context (a job interview, a new situation at work, an internship). In this example one of our clients is invited for the first time to a wedding, and we try to prepare for that situation with a social story:

'This is how a marriage in church might transpire:

Because you are the girlfriend of the brother of the bride, you're brought to the church in a car. Together with your boyfriend, you walk the red carpet towards the church. Usually there are a lot of people on both sides of the carpet. They are curious about what the bride and groom and their families are wearing. Others just want to congratulate the couple.

While walking the carpet you can either look in front of you, or at the people around you. People like you to smile at such a moment. A smile here shows that you are happy.

When the service is finished, people sometimes throw grains of rice at the bride and groom when they step outside the church. Rice is a symbol showing that you wish the couple a nice and fruitful future.'

Scenarios

Finally, we can also use scenarios. To make our future more or less predictable, people make scenarios: if I do this, then the other will do that; if this happens, I might react in this way. People with autism do this much more than others. But they often make mistakes at assessing situations, or they get stuck because they can't think of possible 'good' solutions.

We can help people with this. It can be useful to imagine possible scenarios for a situation. A scenario is a sort of step-by-step plan of a social situation.

L. tells us: 'When I come home, I make a stop at my desk. First, I empty my schoolbag. Then I take whatever I need to the living room. I go there and put these things in their place. After that, I go to the kitchen to wash my hands. Then I go see the dog and say hello. If the dog happens to be in the living room, I can only pay attention to him when I have finished the rest of the scenario.'

A lot has been written about such scenarios. These scenarios are mostly general descriptions, which can be applied to 'everyone'. We like to take things a bit further, based on our solution-focused vision. We expect that people have already discovered many possibilities and resolution strategies themselves. We believe that every situation is different; that every client comes to us with a new and different question, and lives in a different context and has other talents available.

That is why we always choose to produce tailor-made scenarios. To do this, we take into account the client's specific talents and skills. We use these skills and possibilities as our starting point: How did you manage that up till now? What suits you?

Based on this, we write a scenario welcoming what is already there and what fits the personality of the client. We are very concrete about those elements, and we incorporate them into the scenario. Of course, sometimes it is useful to add an extra suggestion, or to correct certain behaviour.

When making a scenario, it is very important to keep the client's goal in mind: What do they want to achieve? What causes them to make the effort to enter an unknown situation? In this way, the scenarios are personal and at the same time future-oriented: to reach your goal you can take these steps and expect those consequences. Thus people learn to cope with known and unknown situations more easily.

D.I.F.F.E.R.E.N.T. – A SOLUTION-FOCUSED GUIDE

In this chapter, we elaborate on what a professional (or any person who supports someone with autism) can do, based on a solution-focused frame of mind. As we said earlier, every therapeutic approach has its own intervention techniques when performing conversational therapy. In the same way, the solution-focused approach relies on some specific methods. Mind that the use of these techniques is not sufficient to expect somebody to work in a solution-focused way.

We are convinced – and like to emphasise this once more – that the basic attitude one adopts when addressing a client can make a big difference and is very relevant. A basic attitude of equality and understanding, and an open mind for the clients' own talents, possibilities, resources and solutions (even though they sometimes seem bizarre), are essential to us.

A solution-focused approach is characterised by a focus on the future and by the particularity of solution-focused questions. Answering these questions demands a lot of creativity and imagination. That is why some people doubt if it is at all possible to work with people with autism in a solution-focused way. But if you understand what autistic thinking implies and how it manifests itself, and if you are able to put the solution-focused scaling and miracle questions (which we discuss below) in such a way that somebody with autism is able to answer them, then you have an approach that works very well, especially with people with autism.

We have imposed a structure on our approach by using the acronym D.I.F.F.E.R.E.N.T. because this embraces the core of what we want to emphasise. For us it is fundamental that one regards persons with autism as people who think differently, with other ideas, values, life targets, needs and solution strategies. Furthermore, we regard them as people with different strengths, talents and ways of making life valuable. It is equally fundamental that this other 'culture' is 'different' for professional helpers, in its most literal sense. Different. Nothing more and nothing less.

If you adopt this attitude when working with people with autism, it means you approach them with respect and curiosity about their strengths, talents and solutions. It also implies that you take the needs and targets of the client into account, that you listen very carefully to what they want. Moreover, this approach assumes an equality of values, goals and needs. Fundamentally different as they may be, they are not to be considered inferior. Every person with autism is first and foremost a human being who in the end has the same needs as every other human being: to lead a life with purpose, to be of importance one way or another, to find a place in society, to be happy.

We are convinced that every professional adopting this basic attitude in their approach works in a solution-focused manner. Based on our experience, we have adjusted some (solution-focused and other) methods specifically to our work with people with autism.

The acronym D.I.F.F.E.R.E.N.T. stands for:

D. Dealing with

I. Increasing competences

F. Finding goals

F. Following your client

E. Exploring

R. Resources and respect

E. Explaining communication

N. Normalising

T. Taking a first step.

These components or methods are continually used in no particular order, like a dynamic anagram.

THE 'D' IN D.I.F.F.E.R.E.N.T.
DEALING WITH

In dealing with people with autism, we like to focus on two points of interest: giving attention and accepting.

Giving attention

Every therapeutic relationship starts by making contact. The therapist will try and develop a relationship with their client. This can happen quickly, or take a lot of time. The importance of a good therapeutic relationship cannot be underestimated. Research[12] shows that 30 per cent of the success of a therapy depends on the relationship between client and therapist.

If you want to make contact with a person, you must approach them without prejudice. You need to have an open mind about their personality, their story, for the kind of help they desire, and sometimes the context in which they find themselves. In making contact and giving attention, the position of 'not knowing' is essential and fundamental to the solution-focused approach. When it comes to their life, the client is the expert, not the therapist. The therapist is only the expert of the therapeutic process.

We don't know what motivates our client, who or what is important to them, what has proven useful up till now, or even what hasn't worked. That is why the therapist should be really curious about the solutions the client has already found or applied.

When you try to make a good connection with your client, an important condition is to speak your client's language. One can only feel well understood when the other speaks the same language and uses similar words and images. Making contact is something that continues throughout the conversation. It happens again and again. So it's not only the first contact that matters. Time and time again, the therapist tries to tune in to the client, constantly trying to listen closely to what is being said, and to understand what could be useful for the client.

Earlier in this book, we wrote that people with autism think in a different way. This implies that they build rapport in another way. In general, we can say that people with autism communicate much more concretely and directly. All social rules that non-autistic people apply when establishing rapport have little meaning to people with autism. We think of 'small talk': going on about this and that, elaborating on trivial issues, etc. These digressions can even cause a lot of stress in people with autism, because it is unclear what kinds of answers this sort of chatter requires.

If we really want to give our attention to people with autism, it should be reflected in our way of building rapport. Trivial subjects are dropped, communication becomes more direct and explicit, we 'cut to the chase' and quickly move on to the topics the client wants to discuss.

This means literally that we often start our conversation with: 'What do you want to talk about today?'

Accepting

Autism causes some restrictions; there is no way around that fact. During therapy, solid psycho/social education appears to help people to recognise what particular restrictions autism causes for a particular person. Based on our solution-focused approach, we try and teach psycho/social education in a more hopeful way. Indeed, hope proves a very important and critical factor for the success of a helping process or therapy. If the client has positive expectations and expects the guidance to help him or her, this hope makes up for 15 per cent of the success of the therapy.

People with autism have received a diagnosis, and that brings many fixed and possible restrictions and difficulties with it. For many of them, this knowledge is paralysing. Yet autism is a dynamic – not static – condition. This means that the client can learn a lot and make substantial changes, provided their resources and possibilities are taken into account.

Together with the client we search for ways in which they already cope with their unique manner of thinking and its consequences. Every client has their own solution strategies, which are very personal. It is the therapist's task to notice these coping mechanisms, to discover them together with the client and to bring them forward.

The next important task for the solution-focused therapist is to accept the solution strategies already used by the client. This is harder than it may seem, because people with autism sometimes make up solutions that seem very bizarre or unusual. Bizarre or not, every solution strategy proves its use and value and comes from an underlying idea or intention.

> W. is a highly-intelligent 35-year-old man with autism. During his years as a student, he tried very hard to live up to the expectations of his surroundings, i.e. his friends, family, teachers. To do so, he often pushed his own limits and felt depressed as a result.
>
> Once he graduated, he started looking for a job. In doing so, it was particularly difficult for him to keep an overview, to communicate and to interact with other people. W. has sensory-processing issues, and he constantly feels overwhelmed by light and sound (he always experiences sound as 'noise').
>
> After various unsuccessful work attempts, he decided that he did not find enough quality of life in living independently. He found it more useful to spend his time in another way and went to live with his mother again. His mother provided him with his daily needs: food, drinks and good advice.
>
> As time went by, he started to exchange day and night; nowadays he is almost entirely nocturnal. He likes the dark and especially the quietness of the night. It enables him to concentrate on what he likes to do: he programmes video games, reads books and listens to his favourite music. Nobody drops in unexpectedly;

everybody else in the house is asleep. His mother accepts his way of life, and notices he is happier that way.

During our coaching conversations, we often talk about the consequences of his choices, especially when it comes to his income. One of the consequences is that he has to see labour inspectors and other official employment services on a regular basis. It takes a lot of his energy to visit these institutions, because they require him to sum up all his restrictions. This gives him a sense of uselessness; it makes him feel like he is unable to do anything and is a burden to society. It takes him a long time to recover from these tests, to get his life back on track and to retrace the satisfaction his way of life gives him. He has to learn to appreciate again what works for him.

Sometimes he also meets with incomprehension, evident in the reactions of his larger family. They think he should get a job, have friends, etc.

He has learned to see and accept this as consequences of the choices he has made. He is at peace with it.

In this example the therapist's task is to redefine what the client thinks others expect from him and also to discuss what skills, talents, interests and possibilities are enhancing the quality to his or her life. The 'D' in D.I.F.F.E.R.E.N.T. thus stands for 'dealing with' or learning acceptance on two levels.

On one level, there is the readiness of the therapist to accept the client as he or she is and moreover to accept the solution strategies they have already developed and to take these for what they are: solutions. This is very important.

On another level, the client has to go through the hard process of accepting they are different: he thinks in an autistic way, he stands in life in a fundamentally different way and, as a consequence, he is faced with a lot of restrictions.

We cannot expect our clients to really accept their restrictions, though. Is it ever possible for someone to fully accept that something is beyond their control, especially a condition that has so many far-reaching consequences and implications? Even more so when it seems 'unfair', compared to all the other people who don't have to live with these consequences?

Because we want to be full of respect for our clients and their difficult task and search for a place in society, we do not talk about merely 'accepting' their being different. We try to give them enough support so that they will be able to deal with the fact that they are different.

THE 'I' IN D.I.F.F.E.R.E.N.T.
INCREASING COMPETENCES
Increasing competences and offering praise

The purpose of a therapeutic or a coaching context is to make the client stronger and more competent, so their life becomes more comfortable. So when a client actively tries and succeeds in making progress, we give them strong affirmations and ample praise. Furthermore, praise helps to improve the relation between therapist and client. And as we have already noted, this relation is of fundamental importance.

Within the context of a solution-focused approach, praise has yet another, more pragmatic dimension: solution-focused praise puts the emphasis on what works well (for this particular client). It helps to point out to the client how their actions help them to reach their goals. It encourages them, provides strength and motivates them to hang on. It gives the client hope that their life will change successfully. Moreover, praise helps to develop the client's creativity and enhance self-esteem: 'If these are qualities I possess, then maybe I'm not so bad after all. I might be able to do some things.'

The aim is to make the client more conscious about the useful things they are already doing and help them on their way to a more comfortable life (whatever that may mean for this particular person). When the client succeeds in seeing this, certain strategies become clearer and that helps them to be able to use them consciously, and thus to gain more control of their life. That is why the therapist compliments the client on everything they have done differently or on what they have tried in the past that has worked out. We validate the client's efforts and ways of handling things.

The therapist is always searching for ways and means to put certain thoughts and actions in a positive framework. This characterises the solution-focused approach. Indeed, our aim is to give our clients a sense of competence.

A mother who has the feeling that she's often nagging her children is likely to be a very concerned and involved mother. She's someone who wants the best for her children and is looking for alternative ways to influence them (otherwise she wouldn't come to see us).

In our coaching conversations, we will say this explicitly: we tell her that she seems to be a very concerned mother to us; it's her choice whether she accepts this new interpretation or not. If she agrees with this, we get an idea of what she thinks is important: for instance being a concerned mother.

From that moment on, it is our task to search – together with her – for ways in which she can handle her children in a sufficiently educative way without being a bore.

When making compliments, we distinguish between direct and indirect compliments. A direct compliment makes the wanted behaviour explicit and praises someone for their achievements.

H. succeeded in having a difficult conversation with his wife. A direct compliment might be: 'You really handled that well and calmly!'

Indirect compliments take a little detour. In this way, you can indirectly express admiration: 'How did you manage to do that?'

Making these compliments by way of a question makes it easier for the client to accept them, because the questions imply a compliment. They force the client to make the compliment themselves, by answering the question. The client searches for what has created results and in which way they have achieved them. In this way people gain insights more easily and are able to see their own possibilities and to reach their goals faster.

An indirect compliment to H. could be: 'How did you succeed in convincing your wife to sit down and listen? What did you do exactly? And then? And then...?'

Despite the advantages of compliments, we have learned from our experience that you should administer them in the right 'amount'. When we listen carefully to our client and search for what goes well or where they make progress, we can quickly notice a lot of elements. This might make us overenthusiastic, which causes us to go too fast for our client. Because autism involves some restrictions, and people rightfully want them to be acknowledged, giving too many compliments too soon and too directly may have an opposite effect, because the therapist might give the impression that they don't sufficiently understand how heavy the burden of living with autism can be for the client.

Next to giving compliments to the client, it can also prove very useful to give compliments to somebody in their surroundings. A lot of people with autism are unable to live without help from other people. In our solution-focused terminology we refer to them as 'external resources'. It is very important for a therapist or social worker to be aware of who these resources are and what they do for our client, and to reinforce them whenever possible.

Note that people with autism aren't always aware of the things people around them do for them, or that they can do some things that might compel the other people in their lives to help even more, or for a longer stretch of time. People with autism find it hard or even impossible to relate to the feelings or experiences of somebody else. Sometimes they aren't at all aware of what others do to make their lives more comfortable. It is only when this is expressed in a most literal way, and when it is explicitly pointed out to a person with autism, that they can see it and respond appreciatively.

Our experience is that the therapist often functions as a role model. Our task is sometimes literally to show our clients how and when to thank somebody, or how and when to give a compliment. At the same time, we make suggestions as to how our client can respond in a way that motivates the other. Consequently, chances grow that this person might do the same things again because now they feel supported. That's how we teach our clients to help themselves.

To people with autism, we have to make explicit the social mechanisms that lie behind actions. We let them practise, and we give direct and indirect compliments on the efforts they make, and we focus on what worked out well. A lot of social skills can really be taught in this way.

THE 'F'S IN D.I.F.F.E.R.E.N.T.
FINDING GOALS/FOLLOWING YOUR CLIENT

Nobody starts therapy without a reason: there is always a complaint, a cause, a wish for change or a goal. To make progress implies hard work. Change doesn't come easily for many people. Therapy is all about change, changing your mind as well as your actions. People with autism don't like change.

The more concrete a desired future or change is made, the more easily it can be achieved. By making the desired situation very concrete, more ideas come up about what can be done to take a step in the right direction. Of course, this does not only apply to people with autism.

When we start up a (solution-focused) helping process, the first thing we do is to define the client's goals. In doing so, we try to determine the desired future as concretely as possible together with the client. Whatever the client indicates as the cause of coming to therapy (a problem, something that bothers somebody else) is our point of departure.

» Why have they come to see us?

» What would they like to change?

» What is it they want help with?

» What is the situation they desire?

» How do they want things to go?

Sometimes it takes a lot of effort on behalf of both the client and the therapist to set these goals straight and concrete. However, we have experienced that, when working with people with autism, there are some goals that seem to reappear.

It is crucial for people with autism to learn to live with their unique challenges. There are a lot of books, movies and websites with ample information on autism. We have experienced people with autism finding it difficult to apply this information to their own situation or life. That is why psycho/social education often takes up a big part of our therapy, coaching or counselling.

People with autism often have a rather limited social environment. Furthermore, autism is an invisible disorder, so people often don't understand what's going on. The public at large only knows the more stereotypical images, but these cannot be applied to every person with autism. That is why professional helpers like us perform a role of listener, sounding board and supporting figure. For some people, the professional worker is (almost) the only person of trust who understands autism (a little).

Sometimes they ask for help merely to keep things the way they are. Some people seek assistance to be able to hold on to what they have. In that case coaching is not about change, but about preservation in order to prevent a relapse.

When the desired situation or the goals of the therapy aren't clear, we have to explore them and make the client express them very concretely. This can certainly take more than one conversation. Some people really don't think at all about what they really want. It takes time. Very occasionally it is the therapist who formulates the goals, after paying careful attention. The solution-focused approach implies that the therapist adapts their procedures to what the client (or their surroundings/context) finds important, what they need or wish.

In order to explore the desired future situation, a specific and widely used method was developed within the solution-focused approach: the 'miracle question'.[13] The miracle question gets the client to think about what they would want in their ideal and therefore desired future situation. A classic way of asking that question is this:

> Can I ask you a rather strange question? What if, after we finish our conversation, you go home, and finish your day the way you always do. Then you go to bed. While you sleep, a miracle happens and all your problems that brought you here today have disappeared. But because you're asleep you don't know this miracle has happened. When you wake up in the morning, what will be the first signs that show this miracle has taken place?

This question requires imagination: we ask the client to imagine in what way their life would be different the day after the miracle has happened. Because imagination is necessary, this question is too difficult for a lot of people with autism. Yet sometimes it works really well. You may be very surprised by the answers you get!

We often notice that people cannot answer right away. They need the time in between two therapeutic sessions to think about it. The miracle question is a very useful one to think about... It is often difficult for people with autism to imagine what a desired situation would really look like. That is why some professional therapists doubt that a solution-focused approach can be successful at all in working with people with autism. They believe it requires too much imagination and focuses too much on the future to be effective with this sort of client.

It is our experience, though, that asking future-oriented questions to a client with autism is indeed very much possible. The solution-focused approach pays a lot of attention to the concrete and the pragmatic. This fits in perfectly well with the autistic way of thinking. A therapist can help the client to find an answer to the miracle question, by asking it in a less 'open' way, and by splitting the desired situation (i.e. the day after the miracle) up into several concrete parts.

» What would you do differently in your job?

» What would you do differently at your desk?

» What would you do differently when you go to the supermarket?

For some people with autism it's impossible to imagine the desired situation. In that case, you can always focus on the past, for example:

» Think about a moment in the past when you thought things were better. What was different then?

» What did you like better?

To picture this situation as tangibly and as clearly as possible, the following questions are useful to explore and concretise:

» What did you do back then?

» How did you do it?

» Who was with you?

» What did the other person do?

» What happened next?

» Who helped you at that time?

These could be followed by some more questions:

» What could help you to make that happen again?

» What helped you in the past?

» In which way did it help you then?

» On what condition would that person help you again?

Mostly the question for help leads to a desire to learn one or more new skills. People realise they have to develop and master a couple of skills in order to reach the desired future. By asking the aforementioned questions, it is quite possible that the clients themselves come up with a skill that could be useful for them to learn.

Because this idea comes from them, because they are the ones to express it, they are very much aware of the reasons why they want to learn it, and they clearly see the advantages the skill might provide in reaching their goal. This motivates them. It is our task not to lose sight of this goal and to help the client with every step they take towards it.

Apart from that, a therapist must be very aware of what this particular client's limits are. What can be achieved and what lies beyond their possibilities? Therefore, a thorough knowledge of autism is essential to us, so we can make a clear distinction between the problems and limitations imposed by the autism (see Chapter 1) for this person.

One of the most challenging tasks in talking to people with autism is to bring order to chaos. Sometimes their autism makes people talk in a very associative way. They change subjects all the time. As a conversation partner, you can help by weaving a thread in what is said, by adding structure to the discussion and maintaining that structure throughout the conversation.

THE 'E' IN D.I.F.F.E.R.E.N.T.
EXPLORING/EXPLAINING COMMUNICATION
Exploring

By asking questions, a therapist is continually exploring while the conversation takes place. To work in a solution-focused way implies that you focus your attention and your questions in a different way than problem-focused therapies. Somebody who works with a solution-focused attitude doesn't look for explanations and causes for problems or how they came about, because they are fundamentally convinced that this will expose even more problems. This doesn't help whatsoever in finding the right direction towards a desired change or what steps can be taken.

When the desired situation becomes clear, ideas and inspiration for realistic strategies and possibilities to improve that situation become apparent. Especially for people with autism, working in a solution-focused way is very useful. Indeed, we have an explanation for the problems they experience. Furthermore, we need to have a clear view of their targets, wishes and desires, because we, with our non-autistic frames of mind, cannot know these at all.

Explore the goal of the conversation

Usually a solution-focused conversation starts off with the 'question of usefulness'. This question is characteristic for a solution-focused approach. It serves as a guideline in stipulating a clear direction and a goal for the conversation. Moreover, in this way the expertise shifts to the client: they are the only one who can know what is needed. We ask our client, 'What would you find useful to discuss today?' or, 'What topic should be brought up today, in order to make this conversation useful for you?'

This shows that we don't assume that the client always wants to start off a new conversation where the previous one ended. People with autism in particular often change subjects. They think and work in a fragmentary and detailed way, as you read in Chapter 1. They often fail to see a 'red line' in their own conversations.

Explore the context of a situation

With each new subject we are challenged to explore the difficulties and/or the context of the situation. Nothing stands by itself, everything is connected. In order to understand the other's story sufficiently, we need as much contextual information as possible. As we said in Chapter 1, people with autism don't see a lot of contextual information. Obviously, this becomes apparent in their conversations, as they tend to describe very little context. That is why a therapist is obliged to ask for it frequently and explicitly.

At the same time, exploring contexts helps us to find resources. Every story reveals resources that are available to the client. The therapist has to label these resources explicitly, so the client gets to understand what may be helpful to them. If somebody knows what it is that is helpful, they are more likely to access those assets in the future. The client can make a choice to actively deploy their resources whenever needed.

The therapist gains a lot by exploring the context of what is said painstakingly:

» It provides an opportunity to give the client compliments on what they've done well.

» It provides an opportunity to clarify which issues are problems and which are limitations due to autism.

» It provides opportunities to find possible solutions for the problems together with the client.

» It provides chances to notice resources and focus on them.

The context of a problem can be explored concretely and meticulously by asking about details:

» What happened?

» Where were you?

» What were you doing?

» Who was there?

» What did the other person do?

» What were the consequences?

Explore exceptions

No problem ever manifests itself all the time and in exactly the same way. There are times when the problem reveals itself to a lesser degree or not at all. This is a fundamental assumption when we work in a solution-focused way. These 'exceptions' to a problem are guides to solutions. That is why we will always focus on exceptions, analysing and investigating them. In the moments when the problem isn't there, when it is less intense or takes less time, something else happens. Maybe our client behaves differently, maybe somebody from their surroundings acts in a different way, or maybe the context changes, by chance or not.

If we succeed in finding out what helped in the past, we can use that information to cope with a future problematic situation in a better way. We also try and take the desired future into account by doing this. What helps our client to reach their target(s)?

This is the search we undertake, together with our clients.

The solution-focused therapist should always look for those moments when things went better, without ignoring or minimising the discomfort the problem causes. Moments of exception are the key to possible solutions and reveal the available resources.

Together we look for concrete circumstances and times when the problem was less prominent.

- » Where were you?

- » What were you doing?

- » Who was there with you?

- » What did the other do?

- » What were the consequences?

» And above all: What would help, so things can be like that again?

Questions such as these require a considerable power of imagination: How were things in the past?

Despite the amazing memory people with autism often have, it turns out that sometimes they find it very hard to answer these questions. And it's not only difficult for people with autism. These questions focus on those details we normally don't pay any attention to. When we face a problem, we do not often take the time necessary to reflect on times when things went (a little) better. Instead, it is our tendency to analyse the problem, to search for causes.

In working with our clients, our experience is that it can be useful to make some helpful suggestions. It often happens that the client 'by chance' tells us about exceptions of the problem. So, if we look for exceptions, we also can fall back on stories other clients have related in previous sessions.

If things need to be more concrete, the therapist can also rely on situations that happen in the context of the conversations they have with the client.

Explaining communication

Because it is often difficult for people with autism to understand language and communication, it is of utmost importance that we communicate in a very explicit way with them. To communicate explicitly means:

» Say what you mean.

» Don't beat about the bush; come straight to the point.

» Communicate concretely.

» Communicate clearly.

» Be transparent.

» Be congruent in what you say and do.

To communicate in a concrete way implies that your language needs to be very clear and unambiguous (see Rule 1 in Chapter 3). People with autism find it easier to understand sentences and questions that are kept short and very concrete. If you want to say or explain something, say it as you think it. Say what you mean.

Therapists are trained to ask open questions. Yet open questions can leave a lot to the imagination, which can make it difficult for people with autism to find an answer to such questions. Closed questions work better. It takes a lot of practice to turn to closed questions and still leave the expertise with the client.

When communicating with people with autism, it turns out to be very important that you are transparent and congruent, meaning that your body language should match what you are saying. This implies that you say what you think, that you put into words what you experience. At the same time, it helps your clients when your non-verbal communication corresponds with what you say. Most of the time they are very sensitive to contradictory signals, which are confusing.

THE 'R' IN D.I.F.F.E.R.E.N.T.
FINDING RESOURCES/SHOWING RESPECT
Finding resources

Notwithstanding all the challenges and difficulties, every human being has some resources. Resources are external or internal possibilities or sources of help. Talents, experiences, possibilities, skills, intrapersonal features, etc. are what we call internal resources. External resources are found in the surroundings: other people, circumstances, possibilities (e.g. financial), spatial or temporal opportunities and so on.

When an individual experiences a problem, he or she will rely on the solution they believe best suited to that moment. When people turn to a therapist for help in overcoming these problems, this means that they have a feeling of being stuck; they don't know what to do anymore; they feel they have run out of options or don't know which choice to make. They are stuck in experiencing the problem, and 'they are forced to...'

People experiencing a problem often don't see a way out, they don't see the options. The way they are doing things is the only way they know: they fail to see possible alternatives. If they did, there wouldn't be a problem.

Yet in every situation there are many solutions, though they may appear hidden initially. Together with the person involved, the therapist has to search for these alternative ways of behaviour or options. To see these options and to have a choice helps the client to again achieve control of their life and of what is happening to them.

To have a better chance of success, it's useful to look for the internal and external resources of a person. We refer to 'success' as an improved condition or a step towards the desired situation. When you have a clear view of your resources, you can think about how to deploy them in order to make a desired change happen. When a client is able to make use of their own resources, they can help themselves. A client can, for instance, find the opportunity to cope with their limitations by asking for help, and by doing so effectively, can activate others to help them.

One way to identify resources is by enquiring how the client may have dealt with a similar situation in the past:

» Have you ever experienced this before?

» What did you do then?

» How did the problem diminish or get resolved?

» Who helped you with that?

Not all situations are the same, so the resources required for this particular situation may be found in a different place. In a solution-focused approach we think of problems and solutions as entirely different and isolated issues. If we keep focusing on the problem and not, for instance, on exceptions, we are unable to see beyond the problem and everything that relates to it.

Human beings can be very resilient, though, and frequently access other resources, consciously as well as unconsciously.

An extensive and often-overlooked source of resources is our thoughts. People cannot turn off their thoughts, they are with us all the time. But we can direct and shape our thoughts to make them more helpful. When supporting people, therapists often notice that the majority of a client's thoughts may not be helpful. Therefore, over the course of time we teach people to think in a slightly different way, so they can see and experience the world differently as well.

Solution-focused therapists train themselves to make positive hypotheses. The reason for this is very pragmatic: it just works better. When the therapist assumes that the other has a good reason to do what they do, it gets easier to develop alternative patterns of behaviour together with the client. And that is the ultimate goal of the therapy.

It is also important to assume that people always have a good reason to do what they are doing. In their own way everybody wants to be successful or significant.

So a person with autism always has good reasons to do something (or not) and so do the people around them. If we assume that somebody acts out of good intentions and if we take those intentions for granted and rely on them to explain the way people act, this indicates that we are looking into what is useful for somebody at that moment. By further investigating these good intentions and asking our clients about them, by making them visible and naming them, together we often find our client's resources and the people who want the best for them (as opposed to people who act in ways that are irritating to others).

This view of people helps therapists as well as clients. If the therapist talks about the way others act in a positive way, the client will also be able to take on this positive attitude.

Some people are very positive by nature, others are rather pessimistic. Quite a lot of people with autism keep many disastrous scenarios in their heads. This is often as a result of negative experiences in the past and can mean that they think that somebody else reacts in a certain way because of something they have done.

There are several interventions we can use to help somebody in making more positive hypotheses. We don't know the intentions of others. Someone may look angry, but this doesn't necessarily mean they are angry. They may have had a bad night, or simply look angry when concentrating, for example. Maybe there was a lot of traffic on their way to work, or maybe their child is sick.

K. drinks very frequently. If we look into this action, we can choose to give it a negative or a positive hypothesis.

A negative hypothesis could be that the client is addicted to alcohol, that she has very little chance of ever recovering. Maybe she is in a bad relationship, or she has a traumatic history; perhaps her parents have an alcohol problem. These are all possible explanations.

A positive hypothesis could be that drinking helps her at times. It enables her to behave in a more social way. Or maybe drinking is just the best solution she can think of at this moment to cope with her difficulties.

This solution-focused vision is fundamental. We assume that people will choose a healthy alternative, once they see that alternative and have it available to them. That is why, together with our clients, we look for these options or solutions that have the same effect.

When a therapist relies on positive hypotheses for themselves, this automatically changes the spirit of the conversation. It changes the way the therapist sees the client. It can change a therapist's perspective of a 'difficult' client. The positive hypothesis forces the therapist to ask different kinds of questions: questions that ask for the motives or the goals of the client. You try and find out how a certain behaviour is meant to help the client reach their goal. In this way and together with the client you can find some possible alternatives in behaviour that suit the client.

This is the reason why we tie our story up to D.I.F.F.E.R.E.N.T., why we think it is so important to view people with autism as 'different' and not as people with some deficit. To regard them as fundamentally 'different' and to have a good understanding of this difference is a positive starting point that results in a positive and constructive attitude for the professional worker. This increases the probability for a useful coaching process.

Finally, it introduces hope, which is an important and critical factor for a successful therapy. If a client can hope for an improvement of their situation or hold onto the hope that the therapy will be helpful, they become more courageous and this puts the client in motion more easily.

Because they see other solution strategies, the client retraces their feelings of control. It gives them a feeling of self-esteem and competence, a belief that 'I'm able to do something!' In this way, our clients master their own situations and can choose to do something else when they want to.

Showing respect

The 'R' also stands for showing respect. A therapist has to respect the life of their client, their achievements and skills, who the client is. In this way, the client feels that you take them seriously and that you value them for who they really are.[14] You don't want the client to change their personality; you want them to change their behaviour.

When people get the feeling that the therapist or professional helper doesn't accept their personality, they offer resistance to the coaching process and they are not prepared to cooperate. We think of this as a very understandable and even healthy reaction.

THE 'N' IN D.I.F.F.E.R.E.N.T.
NORMALISING

Because it is the task of a therapist to support clients in finding solutions for their difficulties and to give them a sense of competence in doing so, it turns out to be important at times to normalise a couple of things. Especially for the people we work with, it can be very important to consider and label some issues they are confronted with as 'normal'. It became apparent for us that people with autism often find it difficult to see that certain problems they encounter are also present in the lives of others. It is very hard for people with autism to project themselves into other situations and to imagine how it would feel for somebody else, or in another context. In order to reach this goal, we noticed in our practice that self-disclosing statements can be very useful for our clients. Narratives (see Chapter 3) can have a similar function.

We often notice that people with autism enjoy the 'normal' contact they have with their therapist. The solution-focused therapist regards them as the expert of their own goals, their own solution strategies, themselves and their own lives. It gives them a positive feeling. The client feels less restricted and temporarily abandons the idea of being 'disabled'.

A lot of people close to somebody with autism want to take care of their autistic relative to such an extent that they start dealing with things in their place. Sometimes they ignore what the person with autism really wants.

THE 'T' IN D.I.F.F.E.R.E.N.T.
TAKING A FIRST STEP

When a client comes to see a therapist, this indicates that there is something that is bothering them. It is our task to find out, together with the client, what they would want to be different. It's a search for a specific target of the client (see Finding goals, above). Once this target is clear and workable, we can look for very concrete steps that can help to set the client on their way to reaching their goal.

The solution-focused approach implies that you begin with an attitude of 'not-knowing'. This means that you follow the client on their way towards the goals they find important, that you try to look in the same direction. In solution-focused terminology, this is referred to as 'leading from behind'. We do not judge how somebody can reach their goals, because we don't know what works best for them, this being another fundamental premise in the solution-focused approach. Only the clients themselves will know which solutions work and which are likely to fail.

When we work with people with autism, we try to make everything as visual as possible. When we talk about taking steps in the direction of the chosen target, Figure 4.1 could be an appropriate image.

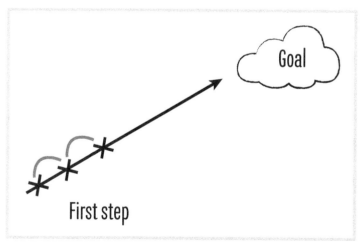

Figure 4.1   Step 1

Sometimes clients don't have ready answers as to which small steps could come next. This requires a certain amount of imagination. When the need is there, when the client asks to be helped, we can go back to their resources:

» What did you do in the past that helped?

» How did you work it out back then?

» And how can we adapt that solution, so it fits the situation at hand?

It is best to keep the first step as small as possible. The smaller the first change is, the easier it is to accomplish. Moreover, it is easier to persevere through a very small change. The client experiences a feeling of success and feels competent. This is, without a doubt, motivating.

We try and formulate this first small step as much as possible in terms of behaviour. We don't refer to someone else's behaviour, but to the way the clients themselves act. Often it is an answer to the question, 'What can I do so that...?'

People can direct their own behaviour, not somebody else's. Everybody is able to choose their behaviour to a certain extent. Moreover, behaviour can be measured: it is very concrete and can be controlled. Thoughts and feelings, by contrast, can be much more elusive, and their consequences are not always as perceptible.

G. is a 40-year-old man with autism. He is a self-employed building contractor. He is a very respected craftsman in the area where he lives, not least because of his meticulous and fastidious way of working. He decided that it would be good to grow and develop his business.

His workload grew so much that he was unable to fulfil all the orders himself. This meant that he needed to make a choice about whether he would keep his business small and only accept jobs he could do himself, or whether he should take on a member of staff. This was not an obvious choice for him. If you employ people, this means that you have to act as a leader, that you have to communicate a lot and plan things. This change created a lot of anxiety and fear.

When I asked him what could be a first small step in the direction of his goal, he said it might be good to include his wife in his business. She had a lot of social skills and really wanted to be a part of his business. This was a relatively safe step for him. Yet this first 'small' step still turned out to be rather big for him. He had no idea how to handle this choice.

As a first small step within this first step, we decided to make a list of all the tasks his wife could do for him. In that way, he could see how things might work. He decided to ask his wife to help him half a day a week with sorting out and arranging files. Once he had taken that step, the next steps followed more easily: his wife started to show up more frequently, got her own computer, started answering the telephone, following up on bills, etc. He noticed this gave him time to do other things. He could make more bids, make up better plans and work without being disturbed by his telephone. After some time, when he had grown accustomed to the new situation, he felt confident enough to take the next step: employ somebody to help in his workplace.

Now, three years later, his company has grown to a small enterprise with three employees besides his wife and himself. By slowing the process down and choosing to take one small step at a time he gave himself enough time to grow in his function as a manager.

In some situations, a first step can be necessary to start learning a certain new skill. Not every person with autism will have enough imagination to think of a possible first small step by themselves.

Roeden and Bannink[15] propose the following step-by-step plan:

Step 1: The coach investigates which skills the client already has that can help to solve their problem. Exceptions, however small, are always there. Skills are (re)discovered and the client can choose to rely on them again.

Step 2: If no or not enough exceptions can be found, the professional can ask the client how others would deal with this problem.

Step 3: If the client is unable to name a solution strategy, the professional can ask the client whether they have any interest in some suggestions the therapist can make to solve the problem. If he does, the therapist can provide examples of how others dealt with a similar problem and what the consequences of their strategies were. To give examples of these, and to expose the solution strategies of other people with autism, add to the motivation and hope of a client. This is because it shows that other people with the same sort of restriction have succeeded in dealing with their problems in a good way.

Step 4: If he or she thinks it necessary, the coach can also give unsolicited advice about a skill that can be learned.

In our therapies we notice that a lot of people with autism have very concrete and practical questions for us. Many of these questions are about planning and organising. People with autism tend to lose their oversight easily, and as a result fail at planning things efficiently.

An example is housework. A lot of people with autism ask for help with this question: 'How can I organise my household in a better way?' Because housework involves a lot of tasks, many people lose sight of what is important and what can wait. Due to a lack of global thinking, people often don't know how to get it all organised. They get stuck in making a practical plan of things in time and space. When we receive a question like this, first we investigate what they are doing and how they are doing it:

» What works?

» What is going well already?

» How do you do those things?

Next, we focus on situations that don't work out that well, and we make them very specific:

» What are all the things you have to do?

» How is your house organised?

» How much time does it take you to do one of the tasks?

» Are there any circumstances in which you did manage to get it done?

Depending on what the client can already do, we search for the first small step towards a better organisation.

Sometimes it is useful to give the client an observation assignment, and to use that as a base to build on:

» Keep score of how much time the different tasks take.

» How much time does it take you to do your ironing?

» How much time does it take to clean the kitchen?

Sometimes we offer something like a very specific step-by-step plan to do chores. Step-by-step plans have the benefit of dividing tasks into several smaller tasks.

For many people, asking for help is a giant step and the 'last resort', because they really don't know what to do anymore. Without a doubt there are a lot of things they have already tried to improve their situation. Sometimes a certain step proved useful, sometimes it didn't.

A much-used technique of the solution-focused approach is asking 'scaling questions'. A scaling question makes the steps that people are taking (or took until now) concrete. It makes people think about what has worked in the past. This should give both the client and the therapist inspiration to find possible next steps. Moreover, a scaling question helps to see difficulties in a more realistic way. People often think in terms of 'always' and 'never'. Reality holds a lot more nuance than that. Looking back to see what is there, everything you did do that helped and what does work (a little), is encouraging and motivating.

A scaling question works like this: 0 stands for the situation with the problem at its worst and 10 stands for your goal. From 0 to 10: Where are you now?

The client gives a number (X). Then the therapist asks:

» What makes you say you made it already to X?

» What makes it X, and not lower on the scale?

» What did you include in the number you gave?

» Who helps you?

» What helps you?

Sometimes the client answers 'o'. In that case, we ask these kinds of questions:

» What helps to make it not even worse than this?

» What makes you get a 0 and not a minus 10?

» Who helps you with that?

» What helps you with that?

When we ask a scaling question, we ask for very concrete actions. We ask for things or people and not so much for feelings. It's easier to control and to name your behaviour than your feelings.

For people with autism it is very useful to make a visual representation of the scale. It helps them to understand it clearly. As we mentioned before, people with autism think in a different way. A visual representation of the question helps them to understand it. We often do it as shown in Figure 4.2.

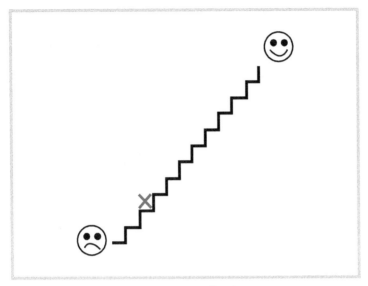

Figure 4.2 Visualisation

After the client has answered the first part of the question, we move on to these next questions:

» Suppose you were at 1 or a tiny bit higher up on the scale, what would you do?

» Suppose you were at 1 or a tiny bit higher up on the scale, what would be different?

» Who would notice you're higher up?

» What would make them notice it?

» Has there been a time you were a ½ or even 1 higher up on the scale?

» What did you do that time?

» How did you do it?

» Who was with you?

» Where were you?

In our experience, it can be hard for many people with autism to answer the question about who would notice things are going better and how they would notice it. A lot of times this question remains unanswered. Yet it is useful to ask. They take it home with them and think further about it there.

Sometimes we turn it into an assignment:

» Maybe you're up to asking this question to your mother, father, partner or a friend?

» Maybe a moment will come when you feel you took a step up the ladder. What do you do then?

» And most of all: What do you notice about the other person? Do they do something else as a result? Do they say something else as a result?

These questions inspire us to think of a possible next small step. They also help us to guide our clients in a very respectful way to their own desired situation.

CONCLUSION

In recent years a growing number of adults with a normal level of intelligence have been diagnosed with autism. Up until now scientific research was mostly focused on the needs and development of children with autism. Wim Stinckens and Anki Vanheeden's research, however, showed that adults with autism often have a lifelong need for support.[16] Yet this does not mean that it always has to be equally intensive. This support is not just psychological or medical; it extends to support within every domain of living: how to spend a day, how to plan free time, how to maintain friendships and relationships, how to find a job.

More and more therapists and other professional workers are visited by people with autism, people who are searching for help that suits them. Professional helpers are confronted with the challenge to start working with autistic people. In this book we have tried to provide a starting point to working with people with autism in a better way. We hope we have succeeded in doing so.

NOTES

1. Isebaert, L. (2007) *Praktijkboek oplossingsgerichte cognitieve therapie.* Utrecht: De Tijdstroom.

2. Bogdashina, O. (2016) *Sensory Perceptual Issues in Autism and Asperger Syndrome: Different Sensory Experiences – Different Perceptual Worlds,* 2nd edn. London: Jessica Kingsley Publishers.

3. Bogdashina, O. (2005) *Theory of Mind and the Triad of Perspectives on Autism and Asperger Syndrome: A View from the Bridge.* London: Jessica Kingsley Publishers.

4. De Shazer, S. and Dolan, Y. (2009) *Oplossingsgerichte therapie in de praktijk, wonderen die werken.* Amsterdam: Hogrefe.

5. De Jong, P. and Berg, I. K. (2004) *De kracht van oplossingen, handwijzer voor oplossingsgerichte gesprekstherapie.* Amsterdam: Harcourt.

6. DSM-5 defines the triad differently: communication and social interaction are mentioned in the same category.

7. Lefevere de ten Hove, M. (2007) *Survivalkit voor leerkrachten, oplossingsgericht werken op school.* Antwerpen-Apeldoorn: Garant.

8. Furman, B. (2006) *De method Kids' skills, op speelse manier vaardigheden ontwikkelen bij kinderen.* Baarn: Nelissen.

9. Erickson, M. H. (2007) *Onbewust leren.* Amsterdam: Karnak.

10. In Chapter 4 we will expand on this process of normalising and focusing on resources.

11. Gray, C. (2010) *The New Social Story Book.* Arlington, TX: Future Horizons.

12. Hubble, M. A., Duncan, B. I. and Miller, S. D. (1999) *The Heart and Soul of Change.* Washington DC: American Psychological Association.

13. Dolan, Y. and De Shazer, S. (2008) *Oplossingsgerichte therapie in de praktijk.* Amsterdam: Hogrefe.

14. Ysebaert, L. (2007) *Praktijkboek oplossingsgerichte cognitieve therapie.* Utrecht: De Tijdstroom uitgeverij BV, pp.52–53.

15. Roeden, J. and Bannink, F. (2007) *Handboek oplossingsgericht werken met licht verstandelijk beperkte cliënten.* Amsterdam: Pearson.

16. Stinckens, W. and Vanheeden, A. (2007) *Onderzoek naar de noden van volwassenen met autisme.* Antwerp: Plantijn hogeschool.

INDEX

'abilities not yet acquired' 41
accepting 61–4
action–reaction process 46, 49
adults with autism 95
attention, giving 59–61

Bannink, F. 88
behaviour, differences in 30–2
body language/non-verbal
    communication 28–30, 49,
    53, 78
Bogdashina, O. 19

communication 25–8
    adapting 46–7, 60–1
    explaining 77–8
    exploring 73–7
    non-verbal 28–30, 49, 53, 78
    and verbal behaviour 30–1
    and visualisation 48–9, 91,
        92
    see also questions
competence(s)
    increasing 64–8
    sense of 83–4, 86
compliments, offering 64–8
concrete notions
    finding goals 68–70, 71–2
    and literal understanding
        25–6, 46–7

and social rules 24–5, 60–1
    see also communication
contextual information 74–5
conversational therapy 50
coping mechanisms 42, 61–3
cultural difference, autism as
    16–21, 22–5
customised services 37

dealing with (D.I.F.F.E.R.E.N.T.
    approach) 59–64
detailed thinking see thinking/
    detailed thinking
diagnosis 33
    advantages and
        disadvantages 38
    usefulness 34–8
    for client 35–6
    for family, friends and
        social work 36–7
    for personal development
        and wellbeing 37–8
    what happens after 38–42
Diagnostic and Statistical
    Manual (DSM-5) 9, 34
D.I.F.F.E.R.E.N.T.
    acronym 59
    approach 57–95
    concept 45